A BOOK ABOUT BUGS

by Virginia Hoppes

© 2017 Virginia Hoppes

**Illustrations by
Hall F. Duncan, Ph.D.**

Book Assembly and Production
Victor Driver, Sr.
Driver Studios, LLC
P.O. Box 1845, Edmond, OK 73083

ISBN-13: 978-1544640402
ISBN-10: 1544640404

First Edition 2017

Published by

Humor & Communication LLC
P.O. Box 7104, Edmond, Oklahoma 73083 USA

A BOOK ABOUT BUGS

Contents

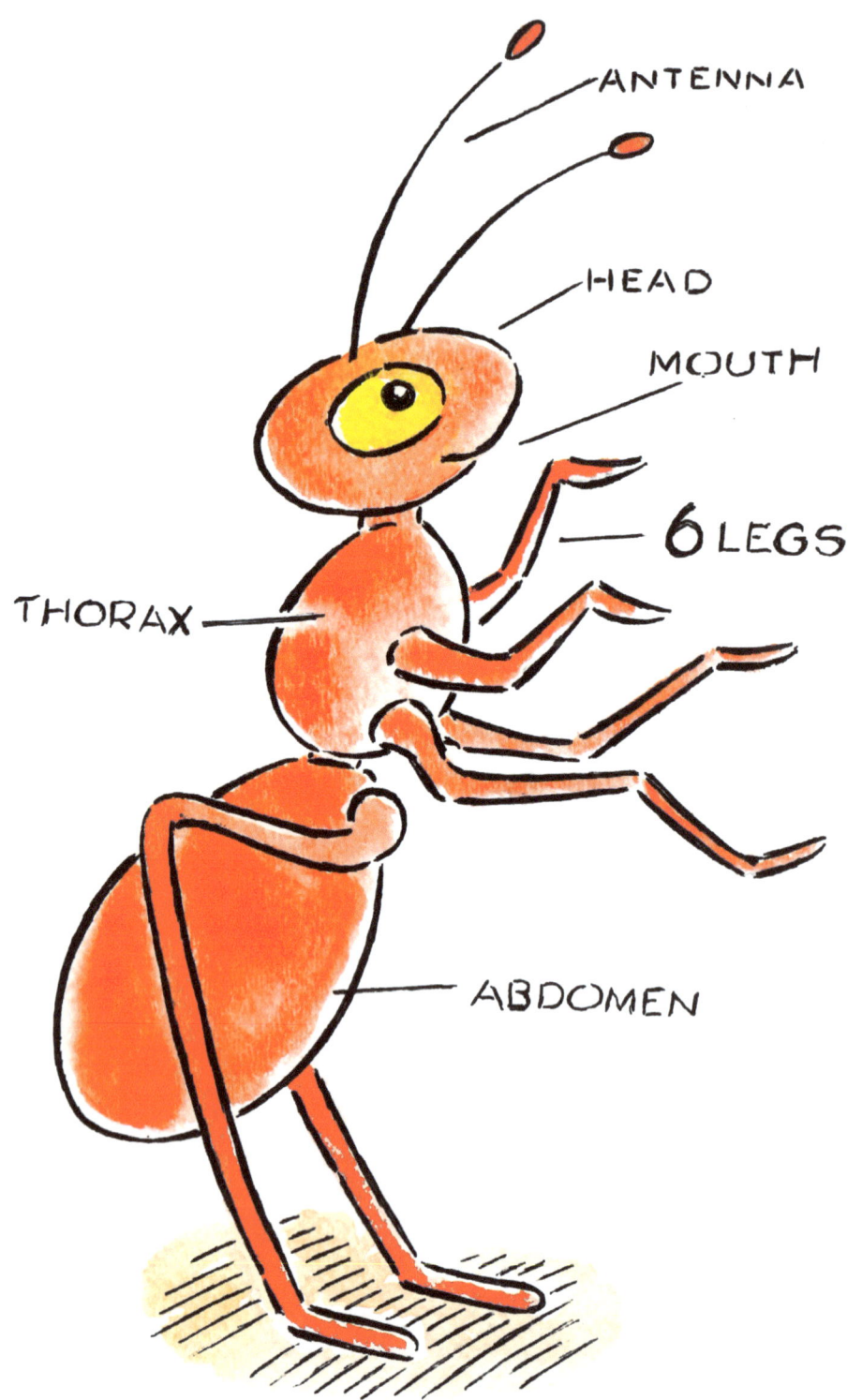

ANTENNA

HEAD

MOUTH

6 LEGS

THORAX

ABDOMEN

What Exactly Is an Insect?

In everybody's yard
there are insects to examine.
The creatures have three parts...
head...thorax...abdomen.

Their heads have tiny, beady eyes
a mouth and funny face.
Some have antenna, looking like
they'd come from outer space.

To be classified as insects
the scientists have said
the creature needs *three* sections...
plus *six* distinctive legs.

A spider doesn't qualify
because it has *eight* legs.
(The extra feet are utilized
to weave fantastic webs.)

Some insects are exotic
like the monarch butterflies
and some are workaholics
like the honey bees in hives.

The busy world of insects
is amazing and has purpose.
Their tiny lives deserve respect.
Let's try not to disturb them.

Dragonflies

Many archaeologists
have documents that show
that dragonflies existed
three hundred million years ago.

Biologists keep studying
these common dragonflies
which have two pairs of sturdy wings
and eighty tiny eyes.

The dragonfly has special gifts.
Its eyes can magnify
the tiny organisms which
become its food supply.

Dragonflies don't use their feet
to crawl upon the ground.
They'd rather stay near ponds and creeks
where they can buzz around.

As they go fluttering through space
up…down…or in reverse
they can hover any place…
the way a helicopter works.

Scientists have shown
in the tests which they perform
some dragonflies have even flown
ten thousand miles or more.

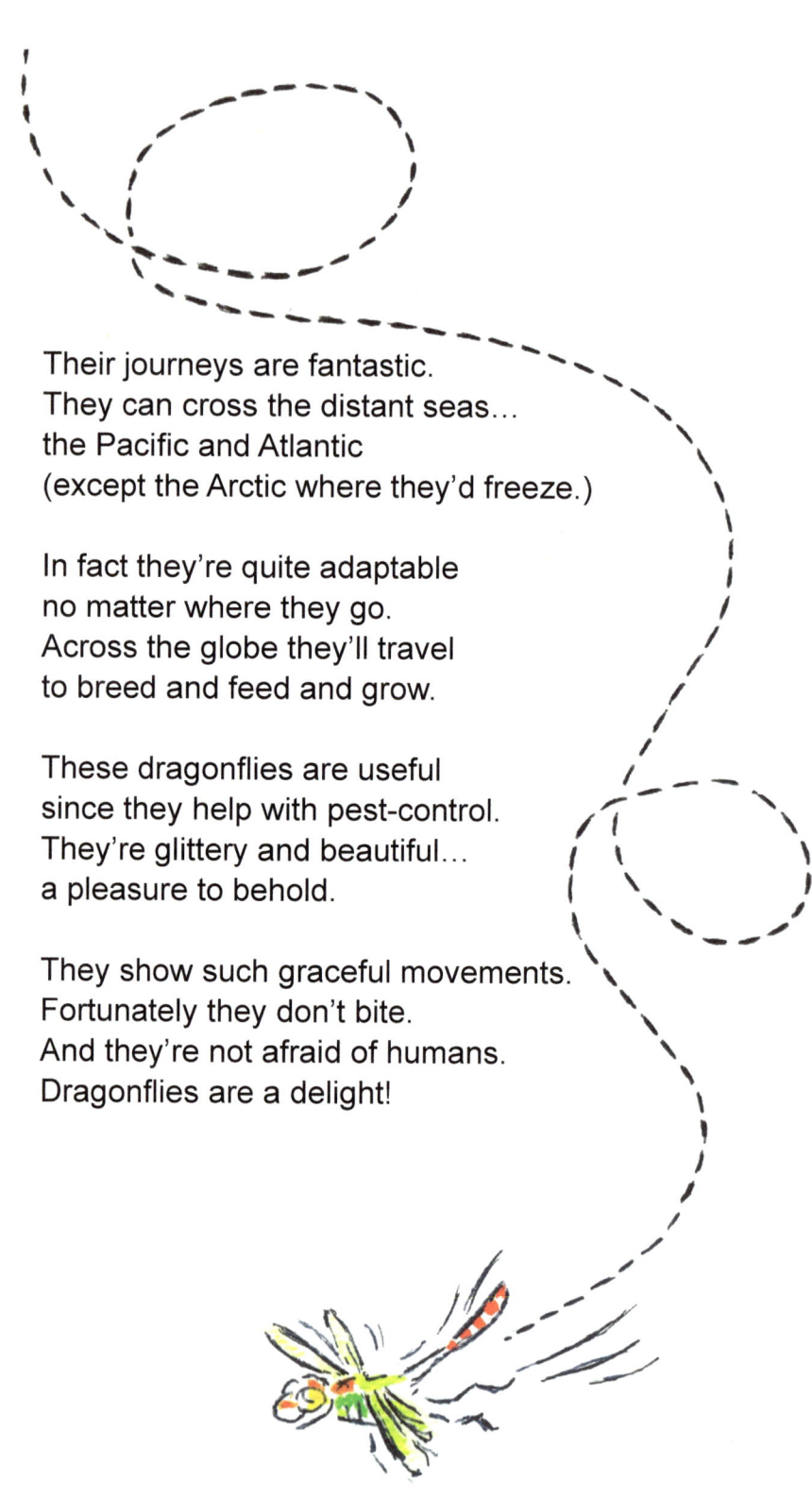

Their journeys are fantastic.
They can cross the distant seas…
the Pacific and Atlantic
(except the Arctic where they'd freeze.)

In fact they're quite adaptable
no matter where they go.
Across the globe they'll travel
to breed and feed and grow.

These dragonflies are useful
since they help with pest-control.
They're glittery and beautiful…
a pleasure to behold.

They show such graceful movements.
Fortunately they don't bite.
And they're not afraid of humans.
Dragonflies are a delight!

Praying Mantis

Mary Ann and Gladys
were walking home from class
and saw a praying mantis
that was crawling through the grass.

Mary Ann was quick and grabbed it.
She put it in a plastic sack
that her little sister, Gladys,
had pulled out from her pack.

Wow! Mary Ann felt lucky.
This praying mantis looked
like photographs she'd studied
in her fourth-grade science book.

The insect was intrIguing.
Gladys questioned Mary Ann,
"Does a praying mantis really
pray the same way people can?"

"I really don't know, honey,
I just don't have a clue.
We need to ask somebody
who would know what bugs can do."

Along came Doug, their soccer coach,
who said he only knew
the way to spray for roaches
and which pesticides to use.

"But girls, I think your plastic sack
needs air-holes…two or three."
He fixed it so the mantis had
more oxygen to breathe.

The girls then saw their pastor
who went jogging everyday.
He'd surely know the answer,
"Can a praying mantis pray?"

The runner noticed Gladys
with the bug and said to her,
"I'm sure your praying mantis
preys since it's a predator.

"Does a mantis *'Pray'* or *'Prey'*?
It's different, you see.
One word is written with an *a*
the other, with an *e*.

"I'd say your little creature
keeps preying (spelled with *e*).
It doesn't have much leisure
and must hunt for food to eat."

Gladys said, "But Mr. Preacher,
it bends its knees and folds its hands.
I'm sure my little creature
prays the way that people can."

Mary Ann then interrupted,
"Gladys, possibly
you are totally mixed up
about that bug's ability."

Yet Gladys kept on saying,
"I positively know,
my bug is praying, (spelled with *a*)
because it told me so."

Mary Ann just rolled her eyes.
"Whatever did it say?"
It said, "I'm praying that you guys
will let me fly away."

Well, that seemed logical enough...
a kind thing they could do
and so the sack was opened up
and out the mantis flew.

The girls ran home without delay
to tell their mom what happened...
the details of their escapade
with the lean, green praying mantis.

Silkworms

Turkish traders had a secret.
Whoever would have thought
that tiny worms were needed
to manufacture cloth?

About five thousand years ago
some Chinese spies were paid
to go to Turkey with the hope
they'd learn how slik was made.

The spies stole silkworms from the Turks
and brought them home but yet…
how could they make the process work?
Now what was the next step?

A Chinese worker had a hunch
that maybe they could use
the soft and sticky substance
formed by larvae in cocoons.

Luckily he found the secret
for making silk in China.
The mysterious ingredient
from silkworms was saliva!

From the spit of silkworm larvae
came the thread which actually
was spun into the garments
which were sold to royalty.

The fabric was so gorgeous
customers would make requests
for the silk to be transported
to the kingdoms farther west.

KIMONO

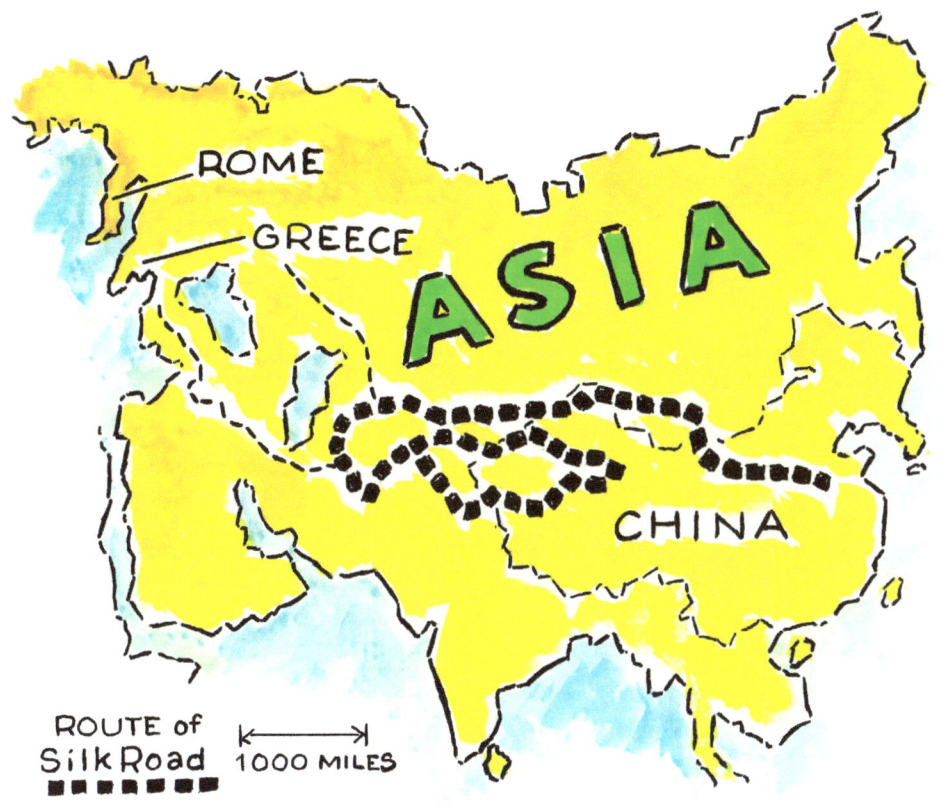

ROME
GREECE
ASIA
CHINA

ROUTE of Silk Road |← 1000 MILES →|

A route known as the "Silk Road"
even crossed the distant seas.
The Chinese sold kimonos
to the Romans and the Greeks.

Silk products became pricey
and as valuable as gold.
Silk once was used as currency
where goods were bought and sold.

Years ago who could have guessed
that silkworms possibly
possessed the power to affect
the world's economy?

Elephants and Bees

In Africa a farmer
was angry and distressed.
Wild elephants had wrecked his yard
and left him with a mess.

The animals had damaged
his gardens and his crops
Why can't these beasts be managed?
Why can't their raids be stopped?

No way the farmer could afford
to build electric fences
or pay for power which, of course,
would add to his expenses.

The farmer heard about the work
of Doctor Lucy King
who'd done some recent research
which he thought was interesting.

She'd studied how the elephants
would freak out suddenly
when they'd detect the presence
of a buzzing honey bee.

If bees are bothered, they have spunk
to guard their colony.
They'll sting the insides of the trunks
of elephants. Ow-wee!

The farmer then decided
he'd surround his land with posts
which held a hundred beehives
to scare elephants…he hoped.

Those bees began to multi-task
producing luscious honey
as well as pollinating plants.
The farmer made more money!

Soon the herds of elephants
by-passed his properties
because they were intelligent
and frightened by the bees.

And now the beehive system
has become a common thing.
Thank goodness for the wisdom
of young Doctor Lucy King.

Millipedes and Centipedes

Said the thousand-legged worm
as he gave a little squirm,
"Has anybody seen a leg of mine?
If it can't be found
then I'll have to hop around
on the other nine hundred, ninety-nine."

It's really not so tragic
since this lowly millipede
has such fantastic magic
it can grow replacement feet.

"Milli" means a "thousand,"
"Pede" is a word for "feet."
A millipede is proud of
its mobility and speed.

"Centi" means "one hundred."
Even though the centipede
is well-equipped, it doesn't
really have one hundred feet.

These worms aren't very loveable.
What value could they be?
Well, they eat bugs which trouble us...
like mites and lice and fleas.

A worm has life-expectancy
depending on its luck
for if it meets an enemy
it's often gobbled up.

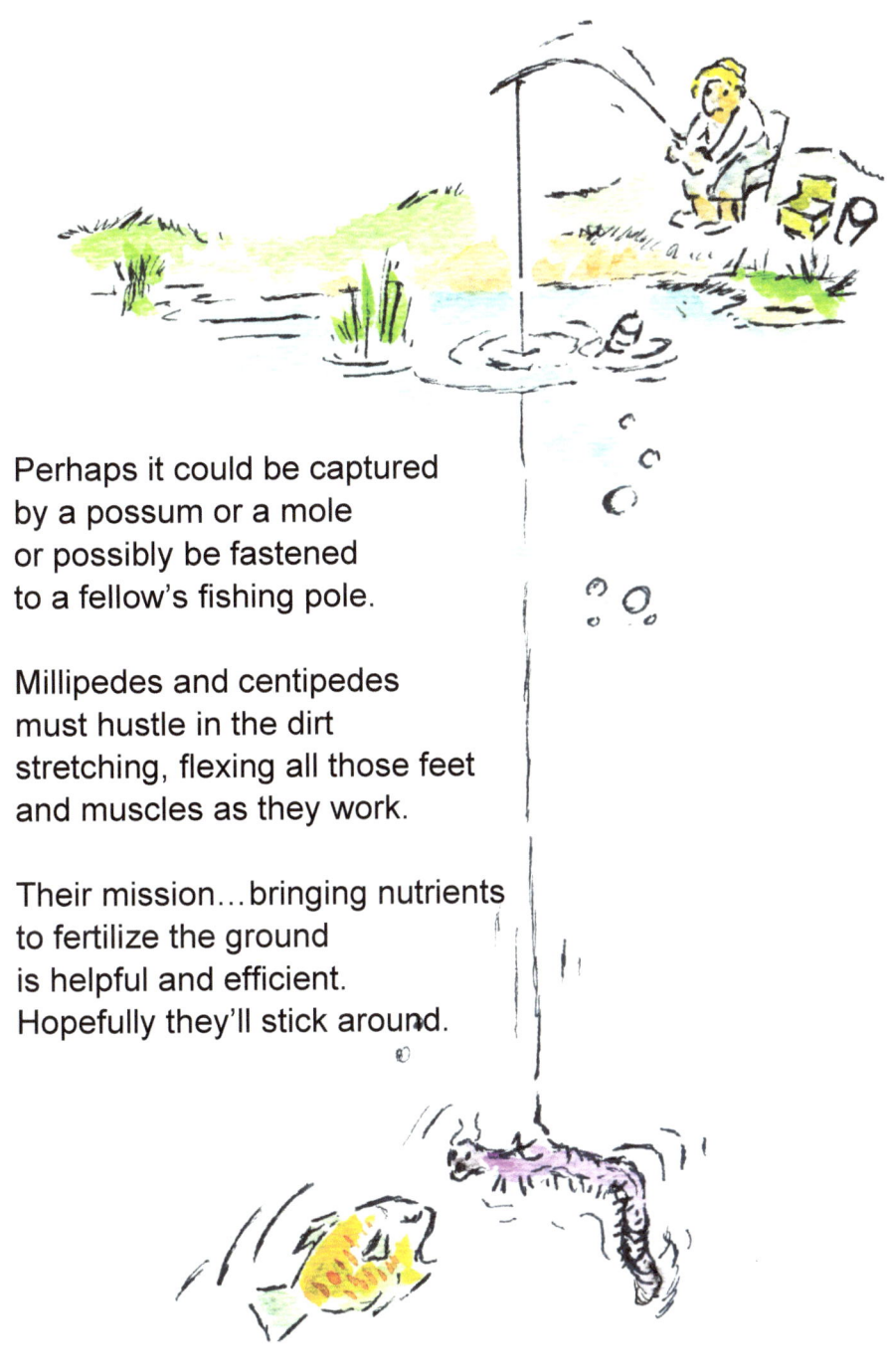

Perhaps it could be captured
by a possum or a mole
or possibly be fastened
to a fellow's fishing pole.

Millipedes and centipedes
must hustle in the dirt
stretching, flexing all those feet
and muscles as they work.

Their mission…bringing nutrients
to fertilize the ground
is helpful and efficient.
Hopefully they'll stick around.

Wooly Worm Song

said a thousand legged worm, as he

gave a little squirm, Has

any - body seen a leg of mine, if it

can't be found, then I'll have to hop around, on the

other nine hundred ninety nine.

Calligraphy by
Dorothy Heidebrecht

Ant Attack!

A little boy named Bert
stumbled on a rock.
He landed on a pile of dirt
on top of ants. Ker Plop!

One ant…two ants…three ants…four
scurrying around…
dozens, hundreds, maybe more
emerged from underground.

It seemed they had a system
like terrorists at work.
They stung the boy and bit him
underneath his socks and shirt.

Ants crawled inside his sweater
and spread into his cap.
Bert realized he'd better
head straight home and take a bath.

He was hurting, he was itching
and he had to get relief.
Those pests continued stinging
without quitting. Ouch! Good grief!

He rushed to take a shower.
The ants which still remained
to pester him were overpowered
and washed right down the drain.

When asked about the ant attack
the lad would tell his buddies,
"The worst part…ants got in my pants!
Don't laugh. It wasn't funny."

A Pet for A Day

Vicky, a fifth grader,
was a little bit upset.
She had to write a paper
and the subject was "My Pet."

But Vicky didn't have a pet.
She hated to admit it
but rules at her apartment said
"No Animals Permitted."

As she walked home that afternoon
she passed a leafy shrub.
She focused on a limb that moved
and saw the strangest bug!

This walking stick was camouflaged.
She thought it looked exactly
like the limb it sat upon…
lean and green and wacky.

She told the bug, "I'll take you
to show my friends at school.
You'll be my pet. I'll name you
'Mr. Twig.' You're really cool!"

At home, she checked the internet
and found some information
so she could write about her pet
and make a presentation.

She learned the bug makes motions
as if blowing in the wind
and if its leg is broken
it could grow another limb.

She fixed a box with rocks and sticks
and put her insect in it.
She hoped the teacher and the kids
would notice her exhibit.

There were stories about their kittens
and a pup and parakeet
but Vicky's friends admitted
walking sticks are more unique.

Mr. Twig was shy and tame...
no buzz, no bites, no stings
and he would never fly away
because he had no wings.

The walking stick cooperated
being a good sport
and Vickie made an "A"...hooray!
for such a great report.

Vickie loved that little bug
but knew he should be free.
She returned him to the shrub
where he'd live happily.

Mr. Twig went undercover
and disappeared from view.
He may have changed his color
the way walking sticks can do.

Vicky said "Good-bye, my friend.
Take good care of yourself.
I hope that we can meet again.
And thank you for your help."

The Hungry Spider

A spider named Spinner
was hungry for dinner.
She went to work weaving a web.
Her body produced
silky thread she could use
to make a magnificent net.

Her creation was elegant
silvery…delicate
sticky like adhesive tape.
When an insect was caught
it got stuck and it fought
but the poor thing could never escape.

Mosquitoes and gnats
flies and chiggers were trapped
and Spinner prepared for the kill.
Each creature was jabbed
with some venom she had…
a method she'd practiced with skill.

The victims were zapped
and they quickly collapsed…
then were wrapped in silk strands
like a mummy.
Oh my! What a feast!
Spinner ate it in peace.
Delicious…nutritious…yum yummy!

At the end of the day
when the web became frayed
the spider did not want to waste it.
Before going to bed
Spinner tore up her web.
It tasted so good that she ate it!

An Aesop Fable
The Grasshopper and the Ants

In ancient Greece, Aesop, a slave,
seemed to understand
the way that animals behave…
like grasshoppers and ants.

Historians were able
to find some manuscripts
describing Aesop's fables.
One story went like this:

A grasshopper was hanging out
one sunny autumn day.
As ants were scampering about.
"Let's stop and chat!" he'd say.

The ants, though, didn't listen
as they carried bits of corn.
They were storing up provisions
while the weather was still warm.

One ant paused for a moment there
and offered his advice.
"Sir, don't you know you should prepare
for winter, if you're wise?"

But Grasshopper decided
that he'd rather sing and chirp.
There'd surely be another time
when he could do his work.

Why work when life is so easy?

WINTER STORE HOUSE

And of course the winter came
as winters always do
with ice and snow and freezing rain.
Grasshopper shivered, turning blue.

He feared that he would freeze to death
or he could starve, perhaps,
while ants enjoyed their cozy nest
and dined and sang and danced.

The moral of the story was:
Make plans. Work hard enough
to be prepared for challenges
that come when life gets tough.

Storytellers through the ages
made additions to the plot.
They described the ants as gracious
and Grasshopper learned a lot.

He was starving and was fed some corn.
He was helpless, tired and frail.
Ants shared their nest and kept him warm.
(That's how some folks told the tale.)

Is it right to make a change
in Aesop's famous classic?
Some listeners might have different tastes
preferring stories that are happy!

Aesop's fables were adapted
for various locations…
tales which people liked to pass
to future generations.

But Aesop never could have known
two thousand years ago
his clever stories would be shown
on movie screens and video.

www.ingramcontent.com/pod-product-compliance
Lightning Source LLC
Chambersburg PA
CBHW050905290526
45792CB00002B/715